# TAKE THE LEAD

## TRUMPET

CW00449500

# Smash Hits

**Series Editor: Anna Joyce**

Editorial, production and recording: Artemis Music Limited • Design and production: Space DPS Limited • Published 2001

IMP

**International MUSIC Publications**

# I'm Like A Bird

Demonstration

Backing

Words and Music by
Nelly Furtado

**Steady pop feel**

4

Demonstration

Backing

# It's Raining Men

Words and Music by
Paul Jabara and Paul Shaffer

**Moderate bright pop feel**

# Lady Marmalade

Words and Music by
Bob Crewe and Kenny Nolan

**Moderately**

9

# Out Of Reach

Words and Music by
Gabrielle and Jonathan Shorten

## Whatever your instrument is...
## you can now

# TAKE THE LEAD

- Each book comes with a professionally recorded CD containing full backing tracks for you to play along with, and demonstration tracks to help you learn the songs

- Ideal for solo or ensemble use - in each edition, songs are in the same concert pitch key

- Each book includes carefully selected and edited top line arrangements; chord symbols in concert pitch for use by piano or guitar

- Suitable for intermediate players

*"A great way to get some relaxing playing done in between the serious stuff"*
**Sheet Music Magazine**

# Discover The Lead

- This new 'spin off' of the Take The Lead series is ideal for beginners of all ages, grades 1-3

- The books contain simplified arrangements of well-known tunes to help the beginner develop reading and playing skills, while increasing confidence as a soloist

- Includes a useful fingering chart plus a CD with full backing and demonstration tracks

- Lots of helpful hints and technical tips to help you get to know your instrument

# SHARE THE LEAD

- All pieces have been carefully selected and arranged at an easy level to provide fun material for today's instrumentalists

- All the arrangements work not only as duets for one particular instrument, but with all other instruments in the series (i.e. the flute book works with the clarinet book)

- The professionally recorded CD allows you to hear each song in 4 different ways – a complete demonstration of the track; part two plus backing so you can play along on part one; part one plus backing so you can play along on part two; and the backing only so you and a friend can Share The Lead!

## A

| | | |
|---|---|---|
| Air That I Breathe, The | TTL | 90s Hits |
| Air On A G String (Bach) | DTL | Classical Collection |
| All Through The Night | TTL | British Isles Folk Songs |
| Amazed | TTL | Ballads |
| Angels | TTL | 90s Hits |
| Ave Maria (Schubert) | DTL | Classical Collection |

## B

| | | |
|---|---|---|
| Bailamos | TTL | Latin |
| Be-Bop-A-Lula | TTL | Rock 'n' Roll |
| Beautiful Stranger | STL | Film & TV Hits |
| Because You Loved Me | TTL | Movie Hits |
| Believe | TTL | Number One Hits |
| Birdland | TTL | Jazz |
| Blue Monday | TTL | Movie Hits |
| Blue Suede Shoes | TTL | Rock 'n' Roll |
| Blueberry Hill | TTL | Rock 'n' Roll |

## C

| | | |
|---|---|---|
| Careless Whisper | TTL | Number One Hits |
| Charlie's Angels | STL | Film & TV Hits |
| Chattanooga Choo Choo | TTL | Swing |
| Cherry Pink And Apple Blossom White | TTL | Latin |
| Choo Choo Ch'Boogie | TTL | Swing |
| C'mon Everybody | TTL | Rock 'n' Roll |
| Coronation Street | TTL | TV Themes |
| Christmas Song, The (Chestnuts Roasting On An Open Fire) | TTL | Christmas Songs |

## D

| | | |
|---|---|---|
| Dance Of The Sugar Plum... The Nutcracker (Tchaikovsky) | TTL | Classical Collection |
| Dancing Queen | TTL | Number One Hits |
| | STL | Chart Hits |
| Desafinado | TTL | Jazz |
| Don't Get Around Much Anymore | TTL | Jazz |
| Don't Say You Love Me | STL | Film & TV Hits |
| Don't Tell Me | DTL | Pop Hits |

## E

| | | |
|---|---|---|
| Everybody Needs Somebody To Love | TTL | The Blues Brothers |
| (Everything I Do) I Do It For You | TTL | Movie Hits |

## F

| | | |
|---|---|---|
| Fascinating Rhythm | TTL | Jazz |
| Flying Without Wings | TTL | Number One Hits |
| | STL | Chart Hits |
| Frosty The Snowman | TTL | Christmas Songs |
| Frozen | TTL | 90s Hits |

## G

| | | |
|---|---|---|
| Genie In A Bottle | DTL | Pop Hits |
| Get Here | TTL | Ballads |
| Gimme Some Lovin' | TTL | The Blues Brothers |
| Great Balls Of Fire | TTL | Rock 'n' Roll |
| Green Door, The | TTL | Rock 'n' Roll |
| Greensleeves | TTL | British Isles Folk Songs |
| Guantanamera | TTL | Latin |

## H

| | | |
|---|---|---|
| Hall Of The Mountain King from Peer Gynt (Grieg) | TTL | Classical Collection |
| Have Yourself A Merry Little Christmas | TTL | Christmas Songs |
| Holler | DTL | Pop Hits |
| How Do I Live | TTL | 90s Hits |
| | STL | Chart Hits |

## I

| | | |
|---|---|---|
| I Believe | STL | Film & TV Hits |
| I Don't Want To Miss A Thing | TTL | 90s Hits |
| | TTL | Movie Hits |
| | TTL | Ballads |
| I Will Always Love You | TTL | Movie Hits |
| | TTL | Number One Hits |
| I'll Be There For You (Theme from Friends) | TTL | 90s Hits |
| | TTL | TV Themes |
| | STL | Film & TV Hits |
| I've Got A Gal In Kalamazoo | TTL | Swing |
| In The Mood | TTL | Swing |
| It Don't Mean A Thing (If It Ain't Got That Swing) | TTL | Swing |

## J

| | | |
|---|---|---|
| Jailhouse Rock | TTL | Rock 'n' Roll |
| Jersey Bounce | TTL | Swing |

## L

| | | |
|---|---|---|
| La Bamba | TTL | Latin |
| La Donna E Mobile From Rigoletto (Verdi) | DTL | Classical Collection |
| La Isla Bonita | TTL | Latin |
| Largo From New World Symphony (Dvorak) | DTL | Classical Collection |

## L cont.

| | | |
|---|---|---|
| Leaving Of Liverpool, The | TTL | British Isles Folk Songs |
| Let's Twist Again | TTL | Rock 'n' Roll |
| Life Is A Rollercoaster | DTL | Pop Hits |
| Little Bit More, A | TTL | Ballads |
| Little Donkey | TTL | Christmas Songs |
| Livin' La Vida Loca | TTL | Number One Hits |
| | TTL | Latin |
| Loch Lomond | TTL | British Isles Folk Songs |
| Love's Got A Hold On My Heart | STL | Chart Hits |
| Lullaby From Wiegenlied (Brahms) | DTL | Classical Collection |

## M

| | | |
|---|---|---|
| Match Of The Day | TTL | TV Themes |
| (Meet) The Flintstones | TTL | TV Themes |
| Men Behaving Badly | TTL | TV Themes |
| Men Of Harlech | TTL | British Isles Folk Songs |
| Millennium | DTL | Pop Hits |
| Minnie The Moocher | TTL | The Blues Brothers |
| Misty | TTL | Jazz |
| More Than Words | STL | Chart Hits |
| Morning From Peer Gynt (Greig) | DTL | Classical Collection |
| My Funny Valentine | TTL | Jazz |
| My Heart Will Go On | TTL | 90s Hits |
| | TTL | Ballads |
| | STL | Chart Hits |

## O

| | | |
|---|---|---|
| Ode To Joy From Symphony No. 9 (Beethoven) | DTL | Classical Collection |
| Old Landmark, The | TTL | The Blues Brothers |
| One O'Clock Jump | TTL | Jazz |
| Oye Mi Canto (Hear My Voice) | TTL | Latin |

## P

| | | |
|---|---|---|
| Peak Practice | TTL | TV Themes |
| Pennsylvania 6-5000 | TTL | Swing |
| Polovtsian Dances from Prince Igor (Borodin) | TTL | Classical Collection |
| Pure Shores | STL | Film & TV Hits |

## R

| | | |
|---|---|---|
| Radetzky March (Strauss) | TTL | Classical Collection |
| Reach | DTL | Pop Hits |
| Rose, The | TTL | Ballads |
| Rudolph The Red-Nosed Reindeer | TTL | Christmas Songs |

## S

| | | |
|---|---|---|
| Santa Claus Is Comin' To Town | TTL | Christmas Songs |
| Say What You Want | DTL | Pop Hits |
| Scarborough Fair | TTL | British Isles Folk Songs |
| Searchin' My Soul | STL | Film & TV Hits |
| Seasons In The Sun | DTL | Pop Hits |
| Shake A Tail Feather | TTL | The Blues Brothers |
| She Caught The Katy And Left Me A Mule To Ride | TTL | The Blues Brothers |
| Sheep May Safely Graze (Bach) | TTL | Classical Collection |
| Simpsons, The | TTL | TV Themes |
| Skye Boat Song, The | TTL | British Isles Folk Songs |
| Sleigh Ride | TTL | Christmas Songs |
| Something About The Way You Look Tonight | TTL | 90s Hits |
| Soul Limbo | TTL | Latin |
| Spring From The Four Seasons (Vivaldi) | DTL | Classical Collection |
| Star Wars (Main Theme) | TTL | Movie Hits |
| String Of Pearls, A | TTL | Swing |
| Summertime | TTL | Jazz |
| Swan, The from Carnival of the Animals (Saint-Säens) | TTL | Classical Collection |
| Swear It Again | TTL | Ballads |
| Sweet Home Chicago | TTL | The Blues Brothers |
| Symphony No. 40 in G Minor, 1st Movement (Mozart) | TTL | Classical Collection |

## T

| | | |
|---|---|---|
| Think | TTL | The Blues Brothers |
| Toreador's Song, The from Carmen (Bizet) | TTL | Classical Collection |

## W

| | | |
|---|---|---|
| When Irish Eyes Are Smiling | TTL | British Isles Folk Songs |
| When You Say Nothing At All | TTL | Number One Hits |
| | STL | Chart Hits |
| | STL | Film & TV Hits |
| Wind Beneath My Wings, The | TTL | Movie Hits |
| | TTL | Ballads |
| Winter Wonderland | TTL | Christmas Songs |

## X

| | | |
|---|---|---|
| X-Files, The | TTL | TV Themes |

## Y

| | | |
|---|---|---|
| You Needed Me | TTL | Number One Hits |
| | STL | Chart Hits |
| You Can Leave Your Hat On | TTL | Movie Hits |

## Take The Lead

### 90s Hits
Air That I Breathe - I'll Be There For You - Something About The Way You Look Tonight - Frozen - How Do I Live - Angels - My Heart Will Go On - I Don't Want To Miss A Thing

### Movie Hits
Because You Loved Me, Blue Monday, (Everything I Do) I Do It For You, I Don't Want To Miss A Thing, I Will Always Love You, Star Wars, The Wind Beneath My Wings

### TV Themes
Coronation Street, I'll Be There For You (Theme from Friends), Match Of The Day, (Meet) The Flintstones, Men Behaving Badly, Peak Practice, The Simpsons, The X-Files

### The Blues Brothers
She Caught The Katy And Left Me A Mule To Ride - Gimme Some Lovin' - Shake A Tail Feather - Everybody Needs Somebody To Love - The Old Landmark - Think - Minnie The Moocher - Sweet Home Chicago

### Christmas Songs
Winter Wonderland - Little Donkey - Frosty The Snowman - Rudolph The Red Nosed Reindeer - Christmas Song (Chestnuts Roasting On An Open Fire) - Have Yourself A Merry Little Christmas - Santa Claus Is Comin' To Town - Sleigh Ride

### Swing
Chattanooga Choo Choo - Choo Choo Ch'Boogie - I've Got A Gal In Kalamazoo - In The Mood - It Don't Mean A Thing (If It Ain't Got That Swing) - Jersey Bounce - Pennsylvania 6-5000 - A String Of Pearls

### Jazz
Birdland - Desafinado - Don't Get Around Much Anymore - Fascinating Rhythm - Misty - My Funny Valentine - One O'Clock Jump - Summertime

### Latin
Bailamos - Cherry Pink And Apple Blossom White - Desafinado - Guantanamera - La Bamba - La Isla Bonita - Oye Mi Canto (Hear My Voice) - Soul Limbo

### Number One Hits
Believe, Cher - Careless Whisper, George Michael - Dancing Queen, Abba - Flying Without Wings, Westlife - I Will Always Love You, Whitney Houston - Livin' La Vida Loca, Ricky Martin - When You Say Nothing At All, Ronan Keating - You Needed Me, Boyzone

### Classical Collection
Sheep May Safely Graze (Bach) - Symphony No. 40 in G Minor, 1st Movement (Mozart) - The Toreador's Song from Carmen (Bizet) - Hall Of The Mountain King from Peer Gynt (Grieg) - Radetzky March (Strauss) - Dance Of The Sugar Plum Fairy from The Nutcracker (Tchaikovsky) - Polovtsian Dances from Prince Igor (Borodin) - The Swan from Carnival of the Animals (Saint-Säens)

### Rock 'n' Roll
Be-Bop-A-Lula - Blue Suede Shoes - Blueberry Hill - C'mon Everybody - Great Balls Of Fire - The Green Door - Jailhouse Rock - Let's Twist Again

### Ballads
Amazed - Get Here - I Don't Want To Miss A Thing - A Little Bit More - My Heart Will Go On - The Rose - Swear It Again - The Wind Beneath My Wings

### British Isles Folk Songs
All Through The Night - Greensleeves - The Leaving Of Liverpool - Loch Lomond - Men Of Harlech - Scarborough Fair - The Skye Boat Song - When Irish Eyes Are Smiling

## Share The Lead

### Chart Hits
Dancing Queen - Flying Without Wings - How Do I Live - Love's Got A Hold On My Heart - My Heart Will Go On - More Than Words - When You Say Nothing At All - You Needed Me

### Film & TV Hits
Beautiful Stranger - Charlie's Angels - Don't Say You Love Me - I Believe - I'll Be There For You - Pure Shores - Searchin' My Soul - When You Say Nothing At All

## Discover The Lead

### Pop Hits
Don't Tell Me - Genie In A Bottle - Holler - Life Is A Rollercoaster - Millennium - Reach - Say What You Want - Seasons In The Sun

### Classical Collection
Air On A G String (Bach) - Ave Maria (Schubert) - La Donna E Mobile from Rigoletto (Verdi) - Largo from New World Symphony (Dvorak) - Lullaby from Wiegenlied (Brahms) - Morning from Peer Gynt (Greig) - Ode To Joy from Symphony No. 9 (Beethoven) - Spring from The Four Seasons (Vivaldi)

# Whatever your instrument is...
## you can now
# TAKE, DISCOVER & SHARE

## Available for Violin

| | |
|---|---|
| 7240A | TTL Swing |
| 7177A | TTL Jazz |
| 7084A | TTL The Blues Brothers |
| 7025A | TTL Christmas Songs |
| 7006A | TTL TV Themes |
| 6912A | TTL Movie Hits |
| 6728A | TTL 90s Hits |
| 7263A | TTL Latin |
| 7313A | TTL Number One Hits |
| 7508A | TTL Classical Collection |
| 7715A | TTL Rock 'n' Roll |
| 8487A | TTL Ballads |
| 9068A | TTL British Isles Folk Songs |
| 7287A | STL Chart Hits |
| 8493A | STL Film & TV Hits |
| 8856A | DTL Pop |
| 9165A | DTL Classical Collection |

## Available for Clarinet

| | |
|---|---|
| 7173A | TTL Jazz |
| 7236A | TTL Swing |
| 7080A | TTL The Blues Brothers |
| 7023A | TTL Christmas Songs |
| 7004A | TTL TV Themes |
| 6909A | TTL Movie Hits |
| 6726A | TTL 90s Hits |
| 7260A | TTL Latin |
| 7309A | TTL Number One Hits |
| 7505A | TTL Classical Collection |
| 7711A | TTL Rock 'n' Roll |
| 8483A | TTL Ballads |
| 9064A | TTL British Isles Folk Songs |
| 7285A | STL Chart Hits |
| 8491A | STL Film & TV Hits |
| 8852A | DTL Pop |
| 9161A | DTL Classical Collection |

## Available for Drums

| | |
|---|---|
| 7179A | TTL Jazz |
| 7027A | TTL Christmas Songs |

## Available for Trumpet

| | |
|---|---|
| 7083A | TTL The Blues Brothers |
| 7239A | TTL Swing |
| 7176A | TTL Jazz |
| 7262A | TTL Latin |
| 7312A | TTL Number One Hits |
| 7503A | TTL Christmas Songs |
| 7507A | TTL Classical Collection |
| 7714A | TTL Rock 'n' Roll |
| 8486A | TTL Ballads |
| 9067A | TTL British Isles Folk Songs |
| 8494A | STL Film & TV Hits |
| 8855A | DTL Pop |
| 9164A | DTL Classical Collection |

## Available for Tenor Saxophone

| | |
|---|---|
| 6911A | TTL Movie Hits |
| 7238A | TTL Swing |
| 7175A | TTL Jazz |
| 7082A | TTL The Blues Brothers |
| 7311A | TTL Number One Hits |
| 7637A | TTL Christmas Songs |
| 7713A | TTL Rock 'n' Roll |
| 8485A | TTL Ballads |
| 9066A | TTL British Isles Folk Songs |
| 9163A | DTL Classical Collection |
| 8854A | DTL Pop |

## Available for Piano

| | |
|---|---|
| 7178A | TTL Jazz |
| 7026A | TTL Christmas Songs |
| 7364A | TTL Latin |
| 7441A | TTL Number One Hits |
| 7509A | TTL Classical Collection |
| 7716A | TTL Rock 'n' Roll |
| 8488A | TTL Ballads |
| 9069A | TTL British Isles Folk Songs |
| 8857A | DTL Pop |
| 9166A | DTL Classical Collection |

## Available for Flute

| | |
|---|---|
| 6725A | TTL 90s Hits |
| 7079A | TTL The Blues Brothers |
| 7235A | TTL Swing |
| 7172A | TTL Jazz |
| 7022A | TTL Christmas Songs |
| 7003A | TTL TV Themes |
| 6908A | TTL Movie Hits |
| 7259A | TTL Latin |
| 7310A | TTL Number One Hits |
| 7504A | TTL Classical Collection |
| 7710A | TTL Rock 'n' Roll |
| 8482A | TTL Ballads |
| 9063A | TTL British Isles Folk Songs |
| 7284A | STL Chart Hits |
| 8490A | STL Film & TV Hits |
| 8851A | DTL Pop |
| 9160A | DTL Classical Collection |

## Available for Alto Saxophone

| | |
|---|---|
| 7005A | TTL TV Themes |
| 7237A | TTL Swing |
| 7174A | TTL Jazz |
| 7081A | TTL The Blues Brothers |
| 7024A | TTL Christmas Songs |
| 6910A | TTL Movie Hits |
| 6727A | TTL 90s Hits |
| 7261A | TTL Latin |
| 7308A | TTL Number One Hits |
| 7506A | TTL Classical Collection |
| 7712A | TTL Rock 'n' Roll |
| 8484A | TTL Ballads |
| 9065A | TTL British Isles Folk Songs |
| 7286A | STL Chart Hits |
| 8492A | STL Film & TV Hits |
| 8853A | DTL Pop |
| 9162A | DTL Classical Collection |

## Available from:

TTL03

## Published by:

IMP

**International
MUSIC
Publications**

**International Music Publications Ltd
Griffin House
161 Hammersmith Road
London
England   W6 8BS**

Registered In England No. 2703274
A Warner Music Group Company

# There You'll Be

Words and Music by
Diane Warren

Demonstration    Backing

# Uptown Girl

Words and Music by
Billy Joel

**Moderate rock & roll**

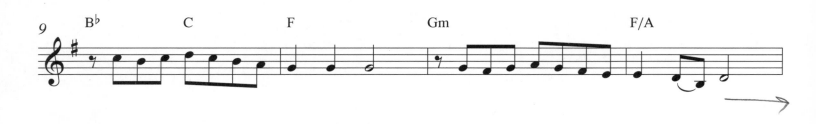

# The Way To Your Love

Words and Music by Mikkel Eriksen,
Hallgeir Rustan and Tor Erik Hermansen

# Whole Again

Demonstration

Backing

Words and Music by
Stuart Kershaw, Andy McCluskey,
Bill Padley and Jeremy Godfrey

**Medium pop**

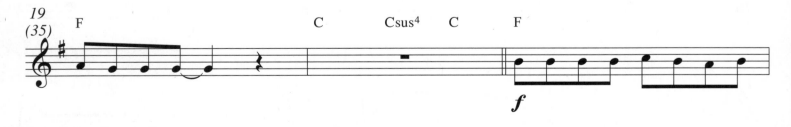

8861A PVC/CD

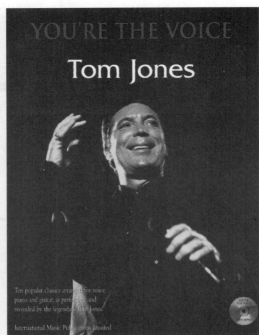

8860A PVG/CD

9297A PVG/CD

Casta Diva from Norma - Vissi D'arte from Tosca Un Bel Di Vedremo from Madam Butterfly - Addio, Del Passato from La Traviata - J'ai Perdu Mon Eurydice from Orphee Et Eurydice - Les Tringles Des Sistres Tintaient from Carmen - Porgi Amor from Le Nozze Di Figaro - Ave Maria from Otello

Delilah - Green Green Grass Of Home - Help Yourself - I'll Never Fall In Love Again - It's Not Unusual - Mama Told Me Not To Come - Sexbomb  Thunderball - What's New Pussycat  - You Can Leave Your Hat On

Beauty And The Beast - Because You Loved Me - Falling Into You - The First Time Ever I Saw Your Face - It's All Coming Back To Me Now - Misled - My Heart Will Go On - The Power Of Love - Think Twice - When I Fall In Love

# COMING SOON: GEORGE MICHAEL

# YOU'RE THE VOICE

## The outstanding new vocal series from IMP

## CD contains full backings for each song, professionally arranged to recreate the sounds of the original recording

# TAKE THE LEAD

## TRUMPET *on these hit songs*

**I'm Like A Bird**
Nelly Furtado

**It's Raining Men**
Geri Halliwell

**Lady Marmalade**
Christina Aguilera, Lil' Kim, Mya and Pink

**Out Of Reach**
Gabrielle

**There You'll Be**
Faith Hill

**Uptown Girl**
Westlife

**The Way To Your Love**
Hear'Say

**Whole Again**
Atomic Kitten

# FEATURES

**On The CD:**

- **full backing tracks, professionally arranged and recorded**

- **full demonstration recordings to help you learn the songs**

**In The Book:**

- **carefully selected and edited trumpet arrangements**

- **chord symbols in concert pitch**

Take The Lead is an integrated series for Alto Saxophone, Clarinet, Flute, Piano, Tenor Saxophone, Trumpet and Violin. In each edition all the songs are in the same concert pitch key, so the different instruments can play together.

All accompanying chord symbols are in concert pitch for use by piano or guitar.

**International MUSIC Publications**

ISBN 1-84328-083-3

9 781843 280835

ISMN M 57021 083 1

International Music Publications Limited
Griffin House 161 Hammersmith Road London W6 8BS England

**Order ref: 9405A**

ISBN 0-7119-3405-3

Wise Publications
Order No. AM91074
ISBN 0.7119.3405.3

## Collect all the other titles in the 'First Guitar' series...

**FIRST GUITAR CHORDS**

More than one hundred
guitar chords, clearly shown
in photographs and
easy-to-follow
chord-box diagrams.
Order No. AM91072

**FIRST GUITAR SOLOS**

Learn with twelve all-time
great pop songs, ranging
from Simon & Garfunkel's
'Scarborough Fair' to
The Beatles' 'Yesterday'.
Order No. AM91075

**FIRST GUITAR RIFFS**

Over sixty guitar riffs,
clearly shown in both
standard music notation
and easy-to-follow
guitar tablature.
Order No. AM91073

---

**Scales In The Open Position...**

C Major
G Major
D Major
A Major
E Major
A Natural Minor
A Melodic Minor
A Harmonic Minor
E Natural Minor
E Melodic Minor
E Harmonic Minor
B Natural Minor
F Major
Bb Major
D Natural Minor
G Natural Minor
E Minor Pentatonic
E Major Pentatonic

**Minor Pentatonic**

A Minor Pentatonic
A Major Pentatonic
B Minor Pentatonic
B Major Pentatonic
C Minor Pentatonic
C Major Pentatonic
D Minor Pentatonic
D Major Pentatonic
G Minor Pentatonic
G Major Pentatonic
D Blues Scale
A Blues Scale
E Blues Scale
Chromatic Scale From E

**Position Playing:
Moving Up The Neck...**

C Major
G Major
A Blues Scale: 5th Position

---

**All the most useful guitar scales, clearly shown in simple guitar tablature
and standard notation with easy-to-follow chord box diagrams.**